Searching for the past

Southern African archaeology series

SEARCHING FOR THE PAST:
the methods and techniques of archaeology

A. J. B. HUMPHREYS

DAVID PHILIP
Cape Town & Johannesburg

First published 1986 by David Philip, Publisher (Pty) Ltd, 217 Werdmuller
Centre, Claremont, 7700, South Africa

ISBN 0 86486 066 8

© text A. J. B. Humphreys 1986
© line-drawings Alixe Lowenherz 1986

Printed by Creda Press (Pty) Ltd, Solan Road, Cape Town, South Africa

Contents

Acknowledgements

I am grateful to the following for generously providing photographs for use in this book: G. Avery and the South African Museum, Cape Town; H. J. Deacon, Department of Archaeology, University of Stellenbosch; T. M. O'C. Maggs, Natal Museum, Pietermaritzburg; A. G. Morris and E. Fuller, Department of Anatomy, University of Cape Town; N. J. van der Merwe, Department of Archaeology, University of Cape Town; H. N. Vos, Stellenbosch Museum, Stellenbosch. Special mention is due to Alixe Lowenherz who was responsible for the line drawings.

I am also grateful to Janette Deacon, Anne Thackeray and Chris Reid for their comments on drafts of the manuscript, and particularly to Margaret Jacobsohn whose journalistic skills did much to improve the text.

What is archaeology?

Moments in time

Scene: Swartkrans, near Krugersdorp, Transvaal
Time: About 2,5 million years ago

The silence is broken by a scuffle and then a series of cries. A leopard stands over the body of an *Australopithecus* ape-man. The victim's friends retreat rapidly for they have no effective weapons with which to defend themselves. The leopard glances around, then sinking his teeth into the back of the head of his prey, he begins to drag it towards a tree. Once in the tree, the leopard devours his kill; a few shattered bones drop out of the tree and become lodged in crevices and cavities in the pitted ground below . . .

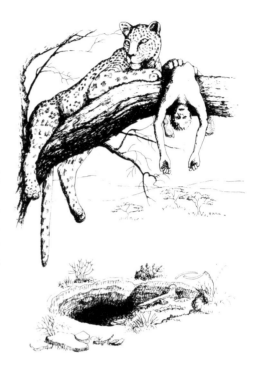

Scene: The mountains around Clanwilliam, south-western Cape
Time: About 2 000 years ago

Summer has passed, there is a nip in the air. The San (Bushman) band begins to feel the diminishing returns from the women's gathering activities. The all-important iris corms — their summer staple — are becoming less easy to find as the plants die off. The usually accessible tortoises are also becoming rarer as they, too, anticipate the onset of winter. The time has come for the San to trek to the coast to exploit the marine resources that will provide a safe food supply for the cold, wet winter

This scene illustrates how, according to C. K. Brain, the Australopithecus *ape-man remains collected in the dolomite caves in the Transvaal. The ape-men did not actually live in the caves, but the bones collected in the underground caverns below crevices in the rocks. Leopards used to prey on the ape-men and probably carried their victims up into trees before devouring them. Some of the bones fell from the trees into the rock crevices below. This reconstruction is based on modern leopard behaviour and also on the fact that some of the ape-men remains show signs of having been bitten by leopard-sized teeth.*

months. Next year they can return to the mountains but now they must begin their migration . . .

Scene: The sand-dunes near Quoin Point, southern Cape

Time: About 2 000 years ago

A very private incident this, for murder always is. A San woman and her baby lie huddled against a dune. A swift arrow, and then another, lodge in the spine of the frightened woman, and the assailant slips away. Who is he? Outraged husband, deceived lover? We shall never know . . .

These scenes are not figments of the imagination: they really did take place. It is the reconstruction of incidents like these, and of the processes of which they are a part, that forms the concern of the archaeologist. The purpose of this book is to explain what archaeology is, and how information about the past accumulates and is preserved, and how ultimately archaeologists recover and interpret this information. All three of the incidents we have just reconstructed are based on solid archaeological research, and our aim throughout this book is to show how we today can gain similar insights into the distant past.

Archaeology as a means of studying the past

Essentially, archaeology is a set of methods and techniques used for making observations about the human past. Archaeology is dependent upon the fact that man is a cultural being and that during the last few million years he has been in existence, man has left material traces which are recoverable by means of archaeological techniques. To understand the methods and techniques of archaeology, it is therefore first necessary to understand what is meant

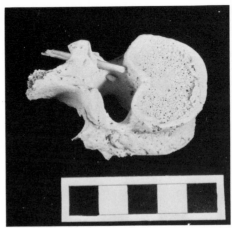

Foul play at Quoin Point? These photographs show a lateral and oblique view of a human vertebra penetrated by two bone points. Both points are typical of those found on Later Stone Age sites. The points themselves may not have caused instant death but any poison would have been fatal. That the victim died as a result of the attack is proved by the fact that there was no rehealing of the damaged bone. (Photograph: A. G. Morris)

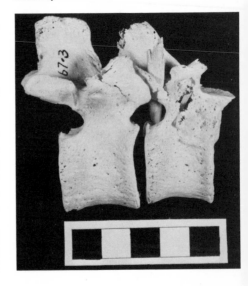

by the statement that man is a cultural being.

The concept of culture is somewhat elusive; dozens of books have been written on the subject without any finality or even consensus having being reached. For the archaeologist culture can be defined as a uniquely human system of habits and customs which stands between man as a biological being and the total environment in which he finds himself. At this point it may be useful to highlight some of the characteristics of this view of culture. In the first place it is important to note that for all practical purposes culture is confined to humans. Moreover, it involves behaviour that is learned; no one biologically inherits culture. Culture is also patterned, in that its various aspects are related to each other in a systematic way. The essential characteristic of culture, however, is that it is adaptive: it enables man to adapt to his natural and social environment. Some archaeologists and anthropologists also talk in terms of 'cultures' when referring to the shared habits and customs of specific societies, much as one might today refer to French culture or German culture.

From this definition of culture, it is clear that both abstract and concrete elements are involved: a religious belief is as much an element of culture as is a clay pot. The problem for the archaeologist is that he cannot recover a religious belief in the same way that he can dig up a clay pot. But this is not to suggest that the religious beliefs of the past are beyond reach. Abstract ideas like political and religious behaviour or kinship relationships may be reflected in what the archaeologist recovers. The material objects excavated by the archaeologists are not 'culture' in themselves but are the products of culture and as such are linked in a systematic way to the cultural system which produced them.

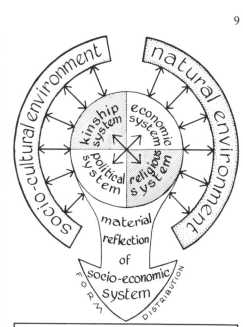

Potential Archaeological Record

This diagram shows how cultural behaviour can be reflected in its material remains. A cultural system, represented by the circle, is made up of various elements such as kinship and religious, economic and political behaviour, all of which interact with each other and with the surrounding socio-cultural and natural environments. This cultural system is reflected in material objects that may end up in the archaeological record. These material objects are the archaeologist's link with the cultural system as a whole.

What interests the archaeologist in his study of past human culture is, therefore, the way in which cultural behaviour is reflected in its material remains.

Three main domains within which archaeological techniques are used should be recognised: prehistoric archaeology, historical archaeology, and ethno-archaeology and experimental archaeology. Although these domains refer to specific segments of

the past or present, the techniques used are similar.

Prehistoric archaeology

As the name implies, prehistoric archaeology is concerned with that part of the human story which lies beyond history and therefore written records. It is by far the largest part of the story because mankind, however defined, has been in existence for several million years whereas the written record extends back only a few thousand years in isolated parts of the world and a mere few hundred years in the rest of the world. This prehistoric section of the human story is recoverable only through archaeological techniques. Examples of studies in prehistoric archaeology range from the early *Australopithecus* or

Contact with the prehistoric past can sometimes be very tenuous indeed. Sometimes a few scattered tools are all that remain. This photograph shows some Earlier Stone Age tools exposed by a moving sand-dune. The tools may be as old as a quarter of a million years. (Photograph: H. J. Deacon)

Restoration work at Blettermanshuis, a typical H-shaped Cape Dutch dwelling in Stellenbosch, provided some interesting information for the historical archaeologist. Excavations revealed evidence of a full-length back stoep with steps that had been razed in the nineteenth century during alterations. It is research like this which enables modern historians and architects to restore old buildings to their original form. (Photograph: H. N. Vos)

ape-man sites to relatively recent San hunter-gatherer camps. In southern Africa the prehistoric period is divided into two main sections: the Stone Age, representing basically the remains of hunting and gathering and herding economies, and the Iron Age, representing more sedentary agricultural populations with a technology that included iron-smelting.

Historical archaeology

The only real difference between prehistoric and historical archaeology lies in the additional element of a written record upon which the archaeologist bases his or her observations about the past. It must be emphasised, however, that this written record may be just as elusive, problematic or misleading as ordinary archaeological evidence. Consider, for example, the biases of political or ideological reporting or simply the desire on the part of an individual writer to make his part in a particular incident appear more honourable or noble. Classical and biblical archaeology are obvious examples of historical archaeology. In South Africa archaeological techniques have been used to study such diverse remains as Lady Anne Barnard's summerhouse in Newlands Forest, Dingane's capital Mgungundlovu, and Anglo-Boer War forts.

Ethno-archaeology and experimental archaeology

This third field is relatively new and consists mainly of the 'archaeological' observations that are being made of existing peoples. The intention here is to study how a human group generates those objects which will ultimately collect to form an archaeological record in the future. Ethno-archaeology and experimental archaeology essentially provide a testing ground for many of the assumptions made about the archaeological record and its relationship to the cultural system that produced it. Studies in this field have ranged from existing San hunter-gatherer groups in the Kalahari to the trash disposal habits of American students.

Relationship to other disciplines

At it is concerned with human behaviour, archaeology has close links with other subjects in the humanities, most notably anthropology and history. It also draws on many other disciplines for theoretical models and practical applications; among these are zoology, botany, geology, geography, chemistry, physics, and even mathematics and computer science. In recent years archaeologists have been prepared to turn to almost any discipline that might provide new insights or new techniques in their quest for information about the past. Many of the inputs from other disciplines will become evident as the various aspects of archaeology are discussed in this book.

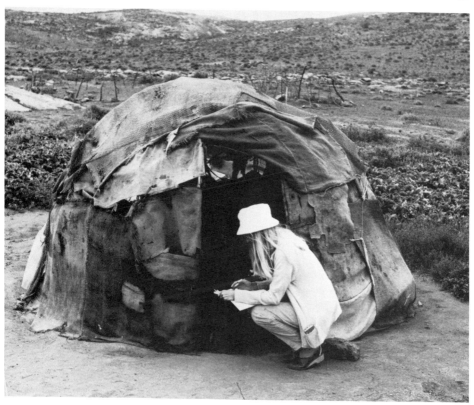

An ethno-archaeologist's task is to make observations among existing people in an effort to throw light on what may have happened in the past. This dwelling in Namaqualand, although made of modern materials, is very similar in style to the matjies huts made by the Khoikhoi in historic and prehistoric times. In the background can be seen the sticks remaining from old abandoned dwellings which are fast becoming part of the archaeological record. (Photograph: H. J. Deacon)

The archaeological record

If archaeological techniques are the means by which it is possible to study the human past, what then is the archaeological record? Briefly, we can say that the archaeological record provides the access to the human past.

What are archaeological remains?

Archaeological remains are basically the material traces resulting from human cultural activity. While these remains are usually objects, it is important to emphasise that the archaeologist is not primarily interested in these objects for themselves even though some of them may well have some intrinsic value. What is important is the relationships in which these objects are found. The study and explanation of these recurring relationships are of the utmost value to the archaeologist in helping him to understand human culture.

The four main classes of archaeological remains that can be found in various and varying degrees of relationship are artefacts, features, ecofacts, and human physical remains.

Artefacts. Artefacts are formed in whole or in part through distinct human activity. They are generally, but not exclusively, objects. Artefacts are, moreover, made up of a series of characteristics or attributes which may be of interest individually or collectively to the archaeologist. Artefacts can range from simple stone tools of little intrinsic value to objects, such as the Mask of Agamemnon, of inestimable commercial and artistic value. But archaeological value need bear no relationshp to intrinsic value, and a simple stone artefact found in the correct context may provide far more archaeological information than a beautiful gold object. It is always the artefact's relationship to something else that is most informative and therefore of value to the archaeologist. A human skeleton is, for example, informative; so, too, are bone arrowheads. But it was the combination of a vertebra and two protruding arrowheads that provided evidence of the sand-dune murder at Quoin Point — and a deeper and different insight into human affairs.

Features. Features are artefacts that cannot normally be removed from the position in which they are found. A burial is a good example of a feature. It may well be possible to remove objects such as a skeleton and grave goods from a burial, but the actual burial itself, which cannot be removed *in toto*, is just as much an artefact. Other features include post-holes, storage pits and hearths. The attributes of a feature can be recorded, as can those of removable artefacts, but the recording has to be done *in situ* by means of photographs, measurements, drawings, etc., rather than in a laboratory. Rock paintings and engravings on cave walls or boulders can also be regarded as features; it is not generally possible to move the art. Photography and careful tracing are required to produce

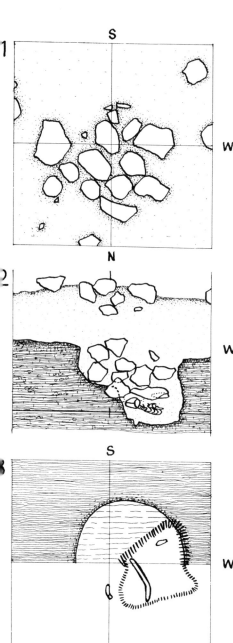

removable versions of the art.

Ecofacts. The term ecofacts is used by some archaeologists to describe a range of objects which, although of natural origin, are deposited in the archaeological record by human activity. Perhaps most important are the faunal and floral remains that represent the animals and plants exploited by man in his quest for food. Such objects may contain far more information than merely man's food preferences; they can also throw light on hunting techniques and proficiency, and seasonal activities.

Human physical remains. Another very important class of archaeological objects includes the physical remains of the people who produced the artefacts with which the archaeologist is primarily concerned. These physical remains usually take the form of fragmentary skeletal material, like the well-known australopithecine remains, but un-disturbed burials can often yield complete skeletons. The study of human remains is generally carried out by physical anthro-pologists, who concern themselves with such matters as physical characteristics, age

These plans are part of the record of a burial excavation undertaken near Koffie-fontein in the Orange Free State. A burial is an example of a feature that has to be destroyed during the course of excava-tion. Fig. 1 is a plan of the surface stone cairn which indicated the existence of the burial. This cairn had obviously to be destroyed if the burial was to be exca-vated. Fig. 2 represents a cross-section through the burial, showing how the body had been placed in a small recess in the bottom of the grave and then covered by more stones. Fig. 3 is a plan of the bottom of the grave once the skeleton had been removed. These sketches, some photographs and a written descrip-tion, as well as the skeleton, are all that remain of this 'destroyed' archaeological site.

and sex, and evidence of disease and dietary patterns — and even, on occasion, prehistoric murders.

Assemblages and sites

These various classes of archaeological remains generally occur in groups or combinations, which are referred to by archaeologists as *assemblages*. The actual point in space where these assemblages or even single objects occur is referred to as a *site*. It follows that the concept of a site is reasonably flexible, ranging from the 'find-spot' of a single object to perhaps a village several hectares in extent. A simple modern example of a small site is a picnic spot where a particularly messy group of people has left a scatter of beer cans, bottles, chop bones and smouldering embers. Such people are the bane of environmental conservation officers' lives, but

Here an archaeologist is carefully cleaning and recording a scatter of animal bones probably left by hunters from the prehistoric past. Note the use of a fine paint brush to expose the bones for photography, and the grid system to locate the finds accurately on the site plan. (Photograph: G. Avery)

in a prehistoric context their activities help form part of the life-blood of archaeology. Some archaeologists may also refer to different areas within an extensive settlement as specific 'sites'. Thus although 'a site' is one of the most widely known archaeological terms, it is a term greatly lacking in precision. For the purposes of the present discussion, 'a site' is taken to mean a discrete bounded spot at which an assemblage or series of assemblages of archaeological remains is found.

The formation of archaeological sites

It is convenient to recognise two factors that contribute to the formation of an archaeological site: *cultural formation processes* and *environmental formation processes*.

Any archaeological site owes its existence in the first place to human cultural activity. Unless a site has been subjected to extreme environmental transformation, as will be discussed later, its very position is a reflection of human cultural behaviour. The activities performed by human beings at that chosen spot will, however, set in train the process of site formation. An archaeological site may represent a single 'incident' in the past, like our picnic site, or it may consist of the remains of a whole series of interrelated events. Consider here the difference, archaeologically speaking, between the simple dismembering of a dead animal and the complexities of even a single day in the life of a village, with its complex web of culturally determined activities. Both situations would contribute to the formation of an archaeological site of a particular kind. The cultural formation processes, then, are the past human behaviour patterns that leave material traces, or archaeological remains, at a particular spot.

Environmental formation processes involve what happens to those cultural remains between the time they were deposited and the time the archaeologist recovers them. An assemblage of artefacts could lie undisturbed until the archaeologist finds it. It is more likely, however, that it will have been subjected to a variety of natural processes, which will have contributed to the partial preservation and modification of the original assemblage. Ideally, the assemblage would have been buried in a deposit, thereby sealing it against such disturbing factors as wind and water action or trampling and scavenging by animals. But the burial of the assemblage may have subjected it to various kinds of chemical weathering or disturbance by burrowing animals or insects. Environmental formation processes can have as great an impact on what an assemblage will look like when the archaeologist finds it as had the actual cultural processes that led to the creation of that assemblage. An archaeological site thus does not represent a 'fossilised' set of prehistoric activities. It is, rather, the result of a complex series of formation processes that have to be unravelled and accounted for before the archaeologist can attempt to interpret prehistoric behaviour.

Primary and secondary context

The recognition of these formation processes has led archaeologists to talk in general terms of sites as being in *primary* or *secondary* context. Primary context sites are those which are believed to have suffered minimal disturbance since they were first formed as a result of cultural activities. Secondary context sites, on the other hand, are those which have been greatly modified by environmental processes — so much so, in fact, that virtually all the original cultural patterns have been obliterated. A simple analogy might be where one's desk top has been tidied by a well-meaning cleaner: all the papers are probably still there but the order and system have been destroyed. An archaeological example of a secondary context site is the occurrence of a few water-worn handaxes among river gravels. These handaxes, being relatively large artefacts, might be the only survivors from what was originally a far larger assemblage. Moreover, they may actually have been made and used many kilometres from the site where they are eventually recovered by the archaeologist. Obviously a secondary context site will be far less informative than a

CULTURAL ACTIVITY

OR

PRIMARY CONTEXT

Debris covered in place by wind-blown sands

SECONDARY CONTEXT

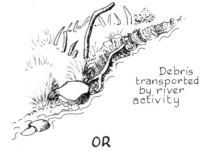

Debris transported by river activity

OR

ORIGINAL PATTERNS PRESERVED

Debris being mined for construction fill

OR
Any of a variety of other processes

ORIGINAL PATTERNS LARGELY DESTROYED

primary context site where handaxes, other artefacts and possibly food waste are found distributed around an abandoned camp site.

Stratigraphy

Archaeological sites do not always consist of one layer or level. Very often sites are stratified, with a series of assemblages lying one on top of the other. Such stratification occurs when a site was occupied intermittently over a long period of time, and is the result of two main agencies: natural deposition and human activity. The archaeologist must be able to distinguish between the two in order to understand the formation of the site. Natural deposition may be caused by such factors as wind or water action. A layer of sand containing no artefacts (referred to as 'sterile' in archaeological terminology), occurring between two layers yielding similar artefacts, might reflect a period of non-occupation during which sand accumulated relatively rapidly. If, on the other hand, the assemblages above and below the sterile sand layer are very different, there are at least two possible explanations. The intervening layer might relate to a long period of non-

occupation during which the cultural system changed quite radically, or it might possibly reflect a hiatus, after which people from another culture occupied the site. Stratification can also occur on a site as a result of human activities. Chief among

This diagram shows the kind of stratigraphy that could await an archaeologist in an unexcavated site. It is the archaeologist's task to unravel this stratigraphy and understand what it means in terms of the history of occupation at the site. This is an essential first step in attempting to interpret the objects which the site may yield. In this example Stratum 1 is the oldest. Stratum 2 is a pit that was dug into Stratum 1; it is therefore younger. Stratum 2 is, however, older than Stratum 3 because it was not dug during the accumulation of Stratum 3 but during the period represented by the interface between Strata 1 and 3; it therefore provides evidence of some activity at the site when there was no longer any more extensive accumulation of deposit. Using similar logic the archaeologist can reconstruct the entire stratigraphic sequence at the site depicted here. (Adapted from W. L. Rathje & M. B. Schiffer, Archaeology, *New York, 1982, p. 192.)*

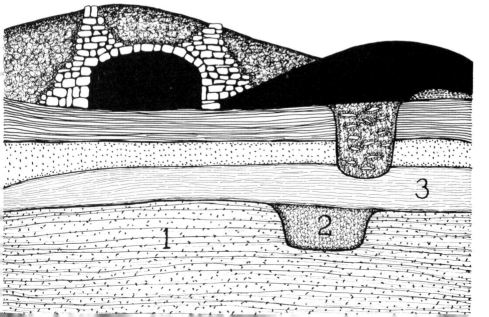

rubbish

2000 B.P. : Stone Age hunting camp (manufacture, use, and deposition behaviour)

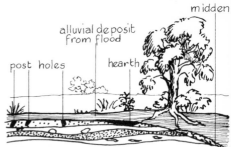

midden

alluvial deposit from flood

post holes   hearth

1800 B.P. : Flood covers remains of camp with silt

rubbish pit

500 B.P. : Iron Age village built on silt (new cycle of manufacture, use, and deposition behaviour)

second alluvial deposit

100 B.P. : New flood destroys farming village; early European house built on new ground surface (new cycles of manufacture, use, and deposition behaviour)

50 B.P. : House abandoned. It begins to disintegrate, forming a mound

This diagram shows how a series of occupations at a site can contribute to the build-up of a stratigraphic sequence representing the various phases of occupa-

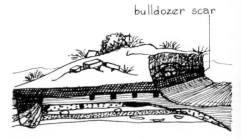

bulldozer scar

PRESENT : Mound is mined for fill to be used in highway construction

tion. (Based in part on R. J. Sharer & W. Ashmore, Fundamentals of Archaeology, *Menlo Park, California, 1979, p. 79.)*

these are construction or demolition, excavation as in the case of burials or rubbish pits, and the disposal of rubbish on dumps (or 'middens', in archaeological terminology).

In broad terms, archaeological stratigraphy observes the geological rule that older layers underlie younger layers, but unfortunately the matter is not always as simple as this because of the human element in archaeology. If people bury a dead person in a cave, for example, it is quite likely that the skeleton will end up next to objects very much older than the burial. The archaeologist has thus to be very careful in his assessment of the degree of association between any objects found within a layer in a site.

The complexity of archaeological stratigraphy cannot be stressed too strongly. Each site is unique, and the assemblages it yields have to be related to each other with due regard for their stratigraphic relationships within the site.

The recovery of archaeological remains

Having established what archaeological remains are and how sites form, we must now focus our attention on how the archaeologist recovers those remains hundreds or thousands or even millions of years after they were first deposited.

The location of archaeological sites

There are three basic ways in which an archaeological site may be discovered. The first is straightforward: the site is obvious and has never been lost. The Great Zimbabwe Ruins would always have attracted attention and have been recognised as an ancient dwelling-place. Large caves or rock shelters are also readily recognisable as potentially inhabitable places.

The second way in which sites are found involves chance or accident. Such activities as quarrying, ploughing, or the erection of buildings can often disturb unsuspected assemblages, structures or burials, and in these cases an archaeologist might be called upon to carry out a hurried rescue excavation. Rescue archaeology is an essential part of the work of most archaeologists, even though the sites which they have to excavate might not be related to any particular research interest.

The third method involves systematic research on the part of an archaeologist in an effort to locate sites which, it is hoped, will contribute to the solution of some or other problem he has formulated. The techniques employed depend upon the types of sites being sought. Highly visible sites like Iron Age stone ruins are readily detectable on aerial photographs, and it is often possible to establish the distribution of a particular settlement pattern by this means before a single site is visited in the field. Aerial photography can also be of use where buried structures or variations in soil chemistry resulting from human occupation give rise to differences in vegetation growth.

Less visible sites such as scatters of stone artefacts have to be located by means of foot surveys. Very often many hundreds of kilometres have to be systematically walked in order to locate the full range of sites in a research area. Wind and water erosion can often expose parts of buried sites. Techniques such as trial trenching, augering or electrical testing of the soil (resistivity survey) can give clues as to what lies below the surface.

In the case of historical archaeology archival research or local traditions can lead to the recovery of sites. The classic example here, of course, is Heinrich Schliemann's discovery of Troy. In South Africa it was historical evidence that led to the identification of Mgungundlovu as Dingane's headquarters.

Excavation of archaeological sites

Digging or excavation is probably the activity for which archaeology is best known. Contrary to popular belief, however, the archaeologist does not simply go out and dig in the hope that something interesting will turn up. Excavation can be a very time-consuming and expensive operation, and it is therefore something not to be undertaken lightly. More important, though, is the fact that all excavation is destruction: every archaeological site excavated is one more archaeological site destroyed. This is inevitable, of course, because the archaeologist cannot remove artefacts or overlying deposit on a site

This Iron Age site near Lindley in the Orange Free State shows how highly visible some archaeological sites can be. It is relatively easy to locate these sites on aerial photographs, and so plot the distribution of various types of settlement pattern. The large enclosure was probably for stock while the smaller structures represent partially collapsed dwellings. (Photograph: T. Maggs)

without systematically destroying that site. It is this realisation more than anything else that makes it impossible for the archaeologist simply to go out and dig sites.

Why dig?

There are two basic reasons why an archaeologist excavates any site. One of these is an attempt to rescue material that may be threatened with destruction. With the ever-increasing tempo of development more and more archaeological sites that have lain undisturbed for perhaps thousands of years are being destroyed by industrial activities such as dam construction, building projects and the opening of new areas for cultivation. The construction in the 1960s of the Hendrik Verwoerd and P. K. le Roux dams on the Orange River flooded nearly a thousand Stone Age sites, and all this information would have been lost if archaeologists had not had the

opportunity to research the area before the completion of the dams.

The second type of excavation undertaken by archaeologists may be described as problem-orientated excavation. In this case the archaeologist decides where to dig on the basis of some or other problems which he hopes to solve. In a relatively unknown area, an archaeologist might be interested in a general outline of the sequence of cultures, and consequently he would initially select a single site with a deep deposit. If, on the other hand, he were interested in how hunting and gathering people used different ecological zones, he would look for a series of more or less contemporary sites in the various zones. In this case he would be particularly keen to

The rescue archaeologist can expect major finds in the most unexpected places. This is a view of the remains of Wagenaar's Reservoir that were discovered in central Cape Town during the construction of a large shopping complex. The archaeologist often has to work under less than ideal conditions to prevent valuable relics being swallowed up by 'progress'. (Photograph: G. Avery)

find sites that not only preserved cultural material but also food waste as this waste would reveal more about how the different environments were used.

Initial recording

Even before the archaeologist begins to excavate, he has a considerable amount of

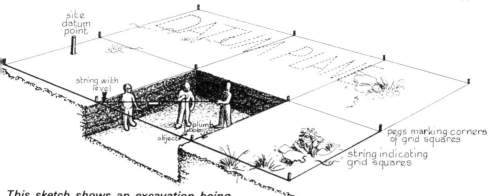

site
datum
point

string with
level

plumb
bob
object

pegs marking corners
of grid squares
string indicating
grid squares

This sketch shows an excavation being undertaken within a grid system. The site has been divided into a series of squares of predetermined size so that the horizontal distribution of objects over the site can be recorded. The archaeologist is also concerned about the vertical distribution of finds within the various strata in the site. In order to record the vertical distribution of finds, everything is related to a fixed site datum point. With careful recording, the archaeologist can reconstruct afterwards the precise positions of everything found in a site in terms of his horizontal and vertical coordinates. (Adapted from W. L. Rathje & M. B. Schiffer, Archaeology, *New York, 1982, p. 193.)*

recording to do. He must locate his site on a detailed map, and plot its position relative to a whole range of factors that may have had an influence on what he eventually finds in the site. These factors might include nearest available water sources, faunal and floral patterns (of particular interest if he wishes to know how the environment was used), and geographical relationships to other sites in the vicinity.

Once on site, the archaeologist has to make a detailed survey of the area. This might involve a contour survey of the ground surface and a plan of any surface features such as stone-walling or scatters of artefacts. One of the main purposes of such a survey is to establish a grid system over the entire site. This grid system provides points of reference for the precise three-dimensional recording of any finds, whether on the surface or in the areas that will eventually be excavated.

Excavation

Excavation usually takes one of two forms or, on occasion, a combination of both. These are *area or clearing excavation* and *penetrating excavation*. In area excavation an extensive area may be cleared to a depth of perhaps only a few centimetres. Such an approach suits the investigation of a large village site, for example, where there was occupation over a wide area during a short time span. Penetrating excavation, on the other hand, involves the investigation of a relatively restricted surface area but to a far greater depth, perhaps several metres. The latter approach is adopted in cave sites where a deep deposit may have accumulated over a period of tens of thousands of years. An ideal, of course, would be to excavate large areas at sites with long sequences, but the time, labour and costs involved usually render this impossible. Thus a penetrating excavation frequently recovers only a small sample of the total archaeological content of a

site, a fact that must be kept in mind when finds are described and interpreted.

When an archaeologist excavates he has to recover his materials in context so that he can attempt to reconstruct the processes that led to the formation of the site. Excavation is therefore carried out with as much care as possible. The main tools used are a small trowel and a brush and pan. All deposit removed is passed through a series of sieves of various mesh sizes to ensure that objects missed during the actual excavation are also recovered. Flotation techniques may be used to float out any tiny plant or bone remains that would have passed through the sieves.

Ideally, the excavation proceeds from one stratigraphic level to the next. These stratigraphic levels are recognised on the

This is an example of area or clearing excavation at Boomplaas Cave near Oudtshoorn. A large area has been marked off in 1 metre squares and the whole area is being stripped systematically a few centimetres at a time. The strings suspended from the roof of the cave permanently mark the corners of each square so that as the excavation progresses downwards the grid system is precisely maintained. In the foreground, partly covered by plastic sheeting, is a hearth feature and a series of pits dug by the prehistoric occupants of the cave. The white layers in the section in the centre of the photograph represent a series of ash layers formed as a result of the burning of dung when the cave was used as a kraal by early herders. (Photograph: H. J. Deacon)

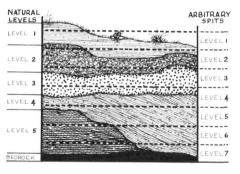

NATURAL LEVELS — LEVEL 1, LEVEL 2, LEVEL 3, LEVEL 4, LEVEL 5, BEDROCK

ARBITRARY SPITS — LEVEL 1, LEVEL 2, LEVEL 3, LEVEL 4, LEVEL 5, LEVEL 6, LEVEL 7

This sketch shows how arbitrarily determined levels in an archaeological excavation could cross-cut the natural stratigraphy in a site. It is clearly desirable to follow the natural stratigraphy during excavation but sometimes the different strata are not at all obvious and the archaeologist has to excavate in arbitrary spits. If this does happen the archaeologist has to be extremely cautious when analysing and interpreting his finds.

basis of subtle colour or texture changes in the deposit. Sometimes, however, the archaeologist is unable to detect any stratigraphic changes, and the deposit is removed in a series of thin arbitrary levels or spits. This approach can produce problems when it comes to analysing the finds because an arbitrary spit could crosscut the natural stratigraphy which was invisible to the archaeologist.

Detailed records are, of course, kept of all stages of an excavation. All finds and

This is a view down a 1 metre square excavation. It goes down about 5 metres in depth and back about 80 000 years in time. It is an example of a penetrating excavation which was carried out at Boomplaas to determine the depth of the deposit in the cave and also to sample its content. Ideally the archaeologist would want to extend the large area uncovered in the previous photograph down to bedrock in the cave but time and money make such large undertakings virtually impossible. (Photograph: H. J. Deacon)

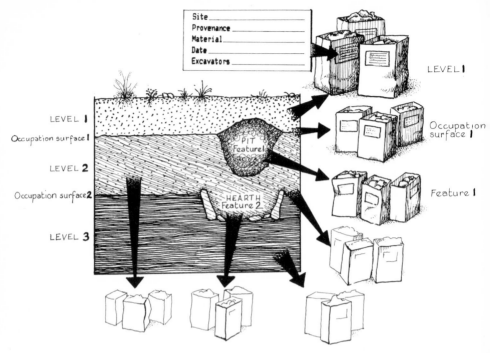

Site_____
Provenance_____
Material_____
Date_____
Excavators_____

LEVEL 1

LEVEL 1
Occupation surface 1

LEVEL 2

Occupation surface 2

LEVEL 3

PIT
Feature 1

HEARTH
Feature 2

Occupation
surface 1

Feature 1

Detailed recording is absolutely essential during any excavation. As objects are removed from the excavation they have to be clearly identified as to their point of origin. If this information is lost, the finds will be virtually worthless. (Adapted from W. L. Rathje & M. B. Schiffer, Archaeology, New York, 1982, p. 190.)

details of the stratigraphy are meticulously recorded on plans and sections and by means of photography. The material finds are carefully packed and bagged according to level and position within the grid system. When the archaeologist finds a delicate or damaged object which would break further or disintegrate as it is removed, he tries to consolidate the object in the excavation before he finally removes it. All features have to be recorded in great detail because not only can they not be removed from the site but, as is most often the case, they have

to be destroyed if the excavation is to proceed to the underlying levels.

Post-excavation procedures

Once the excavation has been completed the archaeologist has to backfill his trenches so as to protect those parts of the deposit that were not excavated. It can happen that future archaeologists may decide to undertake further excavations at important sites in order, perhaps, to increase the size of artefact samples or to seek answers to questions not considered in the earlier excavations. Moreover, methods and techniques are improving all the time, and so it will become increasingly possible to extract more and more information from archaeological sites. The modern archaeologist's disdain for the shortcomings of his predecessors should be tempered by the knowledge that future archae-

1900

1910

1920

1930

1940

1950

1960

1970

A series of motor cars can serve as a modern example of seriation. A motoring enthusiast who knows the sequence of models of a particular make of motor car can, even at a glance, date any car from that series which he might see on the road. Archaeologists similarly attempt to recognise a series within the sequences of artefacts which they study, in the hope that they too will be able to date isolated cases which they find at particular sites. Pots are probably the most suitable archaeological objects for use in seriation. (Adapted from R. J. Sharer & W. Ashmore, Fundamentals of Archaeology, Menlo Park, California, 1979, p. 359.)

ologists will in turn surely regard the present generation in a similar light. It is thus the archaeologist's duty to ensure that his site does not deteriorate any further than it would in the normal course of events had he not excavated parts of it.

The dating of archaeological remains

The dating techniques used by archaeologists can be divided into two categories: *relative dating* and *absolute dating*. Relative dating tells the archaeologist basically that one assemblage is earlier or later in date than another but is unable to determine the exact difference in age or how old either of the assemblages themselves is. Absolute dating techniques, on the other hand, tell the archaeologist, within certain limits, how old the assemblages are in actual years. The following are some of the better-known dating techniques used by archaeologists.

Relative dating

(a) Stratigraphy. The most obvious and common relative dating technique used by archaeologists is stratigraphy. As has already been explained, objects or assemblages occurring higher up in a stratigraphic sequence should be younger than assemblages lower down in the sequence. Being a relative dating technique it is, of course, impossible to establish precisely the actual time relationship between the two assemblages.

(b) Seriation. This technique involves establishing a series of developmental stages in a sequence of artefacts. An example of this approach in modern life would be the development of motor car designs over a number of years. Once a series of changes has been recognised in a sequence, other isolated occurrences can be dated relative to one another on the basis of their respective similarities to the various stages

in the developmental sequence. This technique must, however, be used with caution because not all variations in archaeological objects or assemblages need be related to time. It is possible, for example, that some variations are related to different activities, different sampling techniques during excavation, or simply local stylistic preferences. *(c) Cross-dating.* Often objects of known date can be found associated with assemblages that are undated. If an object such as a coin were to be found in a burial the archaeologist would know that the burial could be no older than the date of the coin and, in fact, might be somewhat younger, because the coin would have been traded or otherwise acquired by the people who buried the corpse. In such a case the coin is said to provide a *terminus post quem* ('a time after which') date for the burial. If a datable object were found in a stratified site overlying an undated assemblage, that object would provide a *terminus ante quem* ('a time before which') date for the underlying assemblage because the earlier assemblage must at least be older than the age of the dated object. In both cases it is, obviously, impossible to establish precisely what the age difference is.

(d) Fluorine. The fluorine dating technique is used to establish whether bones found together are contemporary. Under certain conditions fluorine accumulates in bone as a result of the action of ground-water percolation. Although the amount of fluorine can vary from one locality to another, bones which were deposited at the same time at a particular site should show the same amount of fluorine when subjected to chemical tests. Variations in fluorine content would give an archaeologist good reason to believe that the bones were not 'associated' and that they were brought together through intrusion or some other disturbance of the deposit not readily re-cognisable to the archaeologist. Perhaps the most famous application of the fluorine test was in the exposure of the Piltdown fraud. This celebrated case involved the skilful discolouration and modification of fragments of a modern human skull and an orangutan lower jaw and their placement in an apparently ancient 'archaeological site'. For almost forty years these fragments were accepted as representing a real prehistoric human being, albeit of strange appearance! The fluorine test eventually established that the skull and jaw were not of the same age, and this led to the exposure of the fraud. To this day the perpetrator is unknown and the incident provides a fascinating field for speculation and detective work. In fact the creator of Sherlock Holmes himself, Sir Arthur Conan Doyle, is one of the many people at whom an accusing finger has been pointed.

Absolute dating
(a) Radiocarbon dating. Radiocarbon dating is without doubt the most important and best-known dating technique used in archaeology. It can be applied to anything that once lived: plant remains, bone or shell. The technique depends upon the fact that in the atmosphere both normal carbon-12 (^{12}C) and its unstable radioactive isotope carbon-14 (^{14}C) occur in carbon dioxide. This carbon dioxide is converted by plants into protoplasm, which ultimately makes its way through the digestive processes into animal tissue. Thus the proportion of ^{14}C to ^{12}C in the atmosphere is duplicated in all living plants and animals. When an organism dies, however, it no longer takes in ^{14}C, and what remains in its tissues starts decaying at a fixed rate known as the half-life. The half-life of ^{14}C is 5 568 years, which means that after this period of time half of the ^{14}C atoms in a dead organism will have decayed. Half of the

Radiocarbon dating and stable isotope studies involve complicated laboratory procedures. This is part of a laboratory where research is undertaken into prehistoric dietary patterns based upon the occurrence of carbon-13 in human bones. (Photograph: N. J. van der Merwe)

remaining radiocarbon will decay in the next 5 568 years, and so on. The older the sample the less radiocarbon it will contain, and by measuring the rate of decay it is possible to establish how much ^{14}C remains relative to ^{12}C. From this ratio it is possible to determine the age of the sample in radiocarbon years. Radiocarbon dates are expressed in years B. P. (Before Present), with the present being taken as 1950. The use of this date eliminates the necessity of having to take account of when the radiocarbon date itself was calculated. All radiocarbon dates are quoted with a plus-minus margin of error: this simply represents a small degree of statistical error in the calculation of the date. Radiocarbon dating is generally useful on samples up to about 50 000 years old; samples older than this cannot be dated successfully because the amount of ^{14}C remaining is too small for accurate measurement.

The accuracy of radiocarbon dates has been checked by comparison with dates obtained by dendrochronology (a technique little used in South Africa). Dendrochronology, which involves counting annual growth rings in certain types of trees, is able to establish actual calendar dates back nearly 9 000 years by relating successively older pieces of wood to sections from trees that were felled at precisely recorded dates. Wood samples of precisely known age can then be subjected to

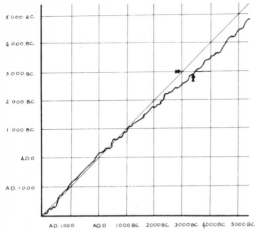

construction of calibration curves, which can be used for converting a radiocarbon date to a calendar date.

When collecting samples for radiocarbon dating the archaeologist has to be very careful to avoid contamination of the sample by any substance containing older or younger traces of carbon because this could result in a completely inaccurate reading.

(b) Potassium-argon dating. This technique, like radiocarbon dating, is based on the decay of radioactive isotopes, in this case the decay of potassium (^{40}K) to argon (Ar). The half-life is, however, somewhat

This graph shows the discrepancy between radiocarbon dates and actual historical dates as calculated on the basis of dendrochronology. The straight line represents the ideal calculated carbon-14 chronological scale while the wavy line reflects discrepancies due to past fluctuations in the amount of carbon-14 in the atmosphere. In the example marked on the graph, a carbon-14 date of 3000 B. C. must be corrected backwards to 3640 B. C.—in short, the carbon-14 gives an age that is actually 640 years too young.

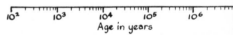

radiocarbon dating so as to check the accuracy of this latter technique. When this was first done it was found that at certain periods in the past there was a discrepancy between the radiocarbon dates and the actual calendar dates established by counting the tree-rings. The reason for this discrepancy was that the amount of ^{14}C in the atmosphere has not always been constant, as had been assumed, and so mechanical calculations of ^{12}C:^{14}C ratios had been producing slightly inaccurate dates for certain periods in the past. This problem has now been overcome by the

This graph shows the potential dating range of some of the more important techniques currently being used. Not every technique can be used in all contexts, but where there is overlap and where more than one technique can be used, the archaeologist can check his dating by comparing the different results obtained. The overlap between dendrochronology and radiocarbon dating allowed for the correction of the radiocarbon time-scale.

longer (1,3 billion years) and the material involved is volcanic rock. The very long half-life means that this technique is useful for dating rocks from about one million years ago to virtually the beginning of time. The potassium-argon technique is perhaps best known for its role in establishing the age of the East African australopithecine remains, most notably 'Nutcracker Man' with his enormous molars.

(c) *Archaeomagnetic dating*. It has been recognised recently that the Earth's magnetic field is not constant and that the magnetic north pole has shifted its position over the years both horizontally and vertically. The course of these shifts over the past few hundred years can be established by studying the orientation of iron particles in certain mineral compounds, such as clay, that have been subjected to high temperatures. This heating causes the iron particles to lose their previous magnetic orientation and realign themselves with the magnetic field existing at the time of heating. The effect of this process is that the new magnetic alignment is 'frozen' in the clay sample. By studying the magnetic orientation in a series of dated samples, scientists have been able to plot the course of the magnetic shifts and so provide a standard against which other undated samples can be compared. As a dating technique, archaeomagnetism does present certain problems for the archaeologist. In the first place, it is obvious that the shifts in the magnetic field will vary from place to place according to the position of a particular area relative to the north pole. This means that there is no universal standard but that a series of local standards have to be developed before the technique can be applied. A second problem is that the samples have to be collected under ideal and very precisely controlled conditions by specialists rather than by the field archaeologist himself. However,

despite these difficulties a start has been made in South Africa with the development of a local standard. Mgungundlovu (Dingane's headquarters) is one site that has been studied because its age is known precisely and it also has hearth features, which provided the heated clay samples.

(d) Other absolute dating methods. There are several other techniques which are less commonly used or which are still being developed. Most promising are *amino-acid racemisation* (based on changes in the amino-acids in bone), *thermoluminescence*, and *fission-track* dating (based on the release of electrons in crystalline or glassy materials).

The acquisition and analysis of archaeological data

Archaeological data as distinct from archaeological remains

Archaeological remains can never speak for themselves. A few chipped stones and a scatter of broken bones are only meaningful to the archaeologist if he abstracts certain information from them. The information from this 'rubbish' (and this is all it often really is) is only intelligible in terms of certain assumptions the archaeologist makes. The archaeologist therefore 'manipulates' the remains in various ways so as to produce his data or information. How, then, does the archaeologist extract this information?

The beginning of analysis: typology

All archaeological analysis begins with the classification of finds or with the development of a typology. The identification (made earlier in this book) of different 'types' of archaeology, or the division of archaeological remains into artefacts, features and ecofacts, represents the beginning of this process. Typological analysis is necessary to bring some sort of order into what would otherwise be an undifferentiated mass of material, and can be carried on to very particular levels of distinction. Objects can be classified according to such attributes as raw material (for example, stone or bone), technique of manufacture, style, form and so on. These attributes can, moreover, be expressed quantitatively or qualitatively in terms of static categories or

as continuous variables. In this section an outline will be given of the various types of classification and analysis used in archaeology.

Analysis of artefacts

Stone

Stone artefacts are probably the most common objects with which the prehistoric archaeologist has to deal. Archaeological sites can yield many thousands of stone artefacts, which have to be reduced to manageable and meaningful categories. Traditionally, the analysis of stone artefacts has been conducted by means of some kind of intuitive typological approach. What this means is that the archaeologist, being accustomed to dealing with specific sorts of

This is part of a typology devised by archaeologist Garth Sampson to analyse some assemblages of Later Stone Age artefacts. It is based on intuitively recognised types, some of which have implications as to assumed use, while others are recognised purely on the basis of form or shape. Numbers 1 and 2, for example, are both end scrapers, probably for working skins, but Number 2 differs from Number 1 in that it has been worked along the sides in addition to the end. It is therefore typologically different. Number 21 is a digging stick weight while Numbers 22 and 23 are upper and lower grindstones.

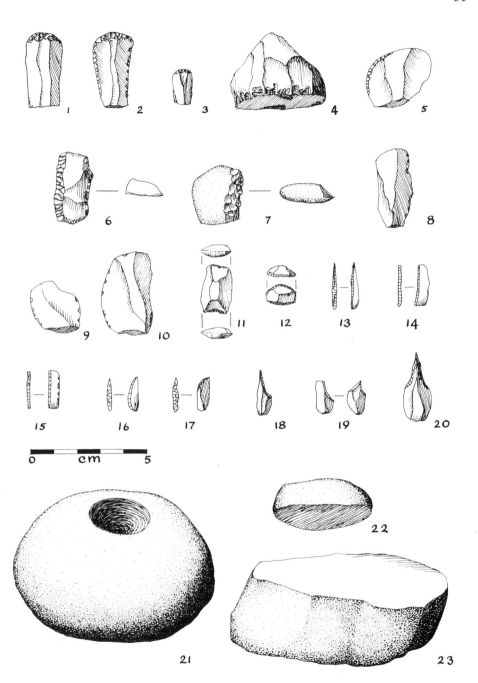

assemblages from limited locations in time and space, has developed some experience of the range of artefacts he can expect, and is therefore able to divide the assemblage into a series of 'types' or recurring forms. These types are generally recognised on the basis of their position in the process of stone artefact manufacture (as, for example, waste material versus finished tool) and on final form or assumed function.

These various types are then named, and the relative frequencies of types occurring are recorded. Assessment of differences and similarities between assemblages (and therefore, by extension, of historical affinity between groups of artefact makers) is then made by a comparison of the occurrence and frequency of certain selected artefact types regarded as being of 'diagnostic' value. This procedure leads to the recognition of different 'types' of assemblages. They are then variously grouped further within larger categories and termed 'phases', 'industries', 'complexes' or 'cultures'.

There are, of course, many difficulties involved in this type of approach, the most obvious being that archaeologists need not exhibit precisely the same 'intuition' when it comes to recognising artefact types. It is, moreover, difficult to decide when one assemblage is different from another in cases where the archaeologist has to deal apparently with continuous variation rather than clear-cut differences in artefact frequencies. As a result of these difficulties, many archaeologists have tried to move away from intuitive typological analysis and have been experimenting with computer-based attribute analysis. In this analysis a variety of characteristics recognised on stone artefacts are fed into a computer in the hope that meaningful clustering will be identified by the computer. Such research has contributed greatly to the archaeological understanding of the gradual and continuous variation that seems to exist through time and space.

In this respect, another approach which has made a significant contribution is the study of micro-wear on stone artefacts. Instead of making educated guesses at the possible function of stone artefacts (and especially those types not used by the few stone tool-using groups which survive in the world today) archaeologists are making use of powerful microscopes to detect and analyse various types of wear on stone artefacts. This wear provides information as to how the artefact was used — such as for cutting or scraping or grinding — and even as to whether the user was left-handed or right-handed! Recognition and analysis of the uses to which artefacts were put may be one way of understanding past human behaviour patterns, without having to resort to the use of arbitrarily recognised types that may bear no resemblance to the concepts that the prehistoric stone-users themselves had of their assemblages.

Pottery

Pottery or at least broken fragments of vessels form another series of artefacts much beloved by archaeologists. Pottery, like stone artefacts, is highly amenable to typological analysis. Various pot-using communities seem to have had very definite ideas about the shape and decoration of their pottery, and these attributes can be readily recognised and analysed. The interpretation of variations in pottery shapes and decorations, as in the case of stone artefact assemblages, is rather controversial, and varying opinions are given as to precisely which attributes or clusters of attributes reflect affinity or distance between the prehistoric groups that produced the pottery.

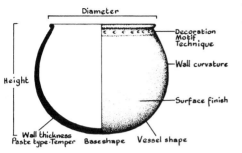

This diagram shows some of the characteristics of a pot in which archaeologists are interested. Every one of these characteristics can vary quite considerably, and it is through the analysis of this variability that the archaeologist can begin to construct developmental sequences or identify different pottery traditions and thereby possibly different cultural groupings. (Adapted from B. M. Fagan, Archaeology: A Brief Introduction, Boston, 1978.)

Metal

The various types of metal objects that survive in archaeological sites can also be subjected to typological description and analysis. These provide information not only about the technology of the people, but, as with an implement like an iron hoe, also of farming techniques. An additional element of interest, however, lies in the analysis of the metal itself with a view to understanding such aspects as manufacture and smelting techniques, and areas of origin of the ore (and, consequently, possible trade routes).

Glass beads

Glass beads, again reducible to different types, are most useful sources of archaeological data. Being small, beads were often traded over great distances, and detailed chemical analysis of the glass can distinguish between superficially similar beads, as well as provide clues as to the ultimate areas of origin of the beads.

Organic materials

Artefacts made from such organic materials as bone, ivory, shell, leather, wood, and fibre often survive in archaeological sites. Some of these artefacts (for example, bone arrow points or ostrich eggshell beads) are readily recognisable with respect to their function, and these objects can be described and analysed typologically. Sometimes leather items of clothing are found, and these objects are usually described individually because their rarity or unique characteristics make them less useful to the archaeologist who is trying to identify variations and trends in the archaeological record.

Analysis of features

Although features cannot be removed from archaeological sites they are nevertheless amenable to attribute and typological analysis. The specific form of a burial, for example the position of the body, may provide clues as to cultural affinity even if there are no grave goods to link the burial directly to any cultural group.

One very important 'feature' of which archaeologists have become aware is the distribution of artefacts over a site. The detailed recording of such distributions can provide clues about activity areas, division of labour, and even, so it has been suggested by some archaeologists, kinship patterns. As emphasised earlier, archaeologists are interested in the relationships between things, and this applies not only between sites but also within sites, where clustering of certain artefact types can be very informative.

Analysis of ecofacts

The analysis of ecofacts can be almost as

informative to the archaeologist as are artefacts. Although they were not created by human beings, their occurrence and distribution in an archaeological site reflect human behaviour patterns.

Fauna

Faunal remains in the form of the bones of animals killed by prehistoric people are often preserved in archaeological sites. These remains, recovered in a systematic way, can yield a wealth of information about past cultural patterns. The first step in the analysis of faunal remains is the sorting of the bone into identifiable and unidentifiable categories. Bone remains on archaeological sites are often highly fragmented, through either human activity or preservation factors. This renders a high proportion of the assemblage unidentifiable, and it is only really diagnostic fragments like the ends of bones or teeth that will allow an archaeologist (or more often a zoologist) to identify the animals represented in the assemblage. Another complicating factor is that a variety of distinctive bones may be used in an analysis, and these different bones could either come from one individual or represent a number of individuals with each bone coincidently coming from different individuals. Because of this problem, when archaeologists come to count the numbers of individuals in each of the species identified, they quote 'minimum numbers' represented. Thus while one springbok horn-core and one springbok tooth could represent two individuals, there is also the possibility that both fragments come from the same individual, so the 'minimum number' of springbok represented is one. On the other hand, two left springbok horn-cores must represent a minimum of two springbok.

The identification and quantification of the species represented in a faunal assemblage can on its own provide a considerable amount of information. The faunal composition may be indicative of the environmental conditions prevailing at the time the site was occupied. The assemblage may, for example, be dominated by either grazing or browsing animals, and this must reflect rather different vegetational conditions. Microfauna such as rats, mice, gerbils and other small mammals are particularly important, as they are extremely sensitive to environmental conditions. To a large extent, of course, the faunal composition of a site reflects human preference and skill in hunting, and this aspect has to be clearly borne in mind when the archaeologist attempts to interpret the patterns underlying the formation of the assemblage.

A further step in the analysis of a faunal assemblage is determining the age and sex of the animals represented. Age is particularly important because apart from reflecting possible cultural preferences, it can also provide leads as to the season of the year the site was occupied. For example, it was discovered in the Western Cape site of De Hangen that the vast majority of the dassies represented here were killed between the ages of 6 and 7 months. Dassies have a very limited birth season — between late September and early November — and so by means of a simple calculation archaeologists were able to determine that De Hangen must have been occupied at least during the approximate period of February to April for the age distribution of the dassies represented at the site to have occurred as it did. It is evidence like this which enables archaeologists to reconstruct annual seasonal movements, as in the case of the Clanwilliam incident mentioned at the beginning of the book.

Another important though somewhat elusive question that can be studied through faunal remains is when and how

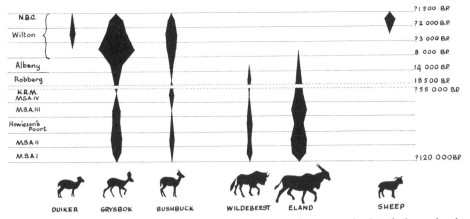

		?1500 B.P.
N.B.C.		?2000 B.P.
Wilton		?3000 B.P.
		8000 B.P.
Albany		14000 B.P.
Robberg		18500 B.P.
K.R.M. MSA.IV		?55000 B.P.
MSA.III		
Howieson's Poort		
MSA.II		
MSA.I		?120000 B.P.

DUIKER   GRYSBOK   BUSHBUCK   WILDEBEEST   ELAND   SHEEP

This diagram, adapted from the work of R. G. Klein, shows changes through time in the occurrence of selected animal species as identified in two sites located along the southern Cape coast: Nelson Bay Cave (NBC) and Klasies River Mouth (KRM). The two sequences together cover a period of about 120 000 years. The relatively large numbers of duiker, grysbok and bushbuck during the last 8 000 years suggest an environment very similar to that existing today. In Middle Stone Age (MSA) times, however, the environment was very different. Wildebeest and eland suggest that a grassland environment must have existed then. The gradual disappearance of these animals points to their withdrawal from the area as forests began to develop. The very late appearance of sheep from about 2 000 years ago represents the arrival in the area of the first herders of domesticated animals.

man started to domesticate animals and so begin to adopt a pastoral way of life. This is difficult to determine because apart from the problem of distinguishing between wild and domesticated animals of similar size (for example, a wildebeest versus a cow — this, of course, on the basis of a few small bone fragments!), there is also the fact that man must have manipulated the animals concerned for a considerable period of time before the physical features that would distinguish the animal as 'domesticated' could be expected to emerge.

The study of the carbon-13 (^{13}C) content of bone can provide information about the type of plant food which that person or animal ate during the last years of its life. The amount of ^{13}C in the bone is an index of the ^{13}C content of the plants consumed. In the early 1970s it was discovered that not all plants photosynthetise carbon dioxide in the same way. There are two distinct processes, known as the C_3 and C_4 pathways, which relate to the types of carbon molecules formed during the initial stages of photosynthesis. It has been found that all trees, most shrubs, and temperate grasses use the C_3 pathway whereas the grasses and shrubs of hotter arid zones use the C_4 pathway. What is important is that the ^{13}C content of C_3 plants is significantly less than that of C_4 plants. This means that if people living in a predominantly C_3 plant environment obtained access to a C_4 plant which became a dietary staple, the relative importance of this new plant would be reflected in the amount of ^{13}C in their bones. Maize, sorghum and millet are all C_4 plants, and it is thus possible to trace their diffusion into

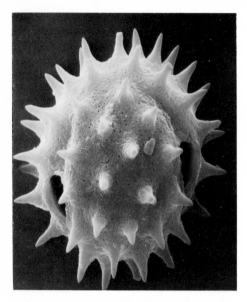

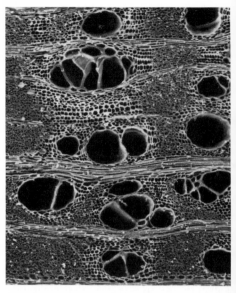

areas dominated by C₃ plants. This technique is relatively new but there is little doubt that it holds out exciting prospects for research.

Flora

Floral or botanical remains are much rarer and more difficult to recover from archaeological sites. Clearly, such delicate material is far less likely to remain preserved in archaeological sites. Archaeologists, however, recognise the importance of this material, and often go to great lengths to recover whatever botanical remains have survived. As mentioned earlier, flotation techniques, by which the light plant remains are floated· out of the samples of deposit, are widely used.

The most durable plant remains that survive in archaeological sites are pollen. These tiny grains can be recovered, and because plants have very distinctive types of pollen it is possible for specialists to identify the various kinds of pollen-producing plants that must have existed in the

Pollen grains are very hardy and survive for long periods of time in archaeological sites. They are also very distinctive and can be readily identified. The first photograph is a pollen grain from a plant of the daisy, or Compositae, family that has been enlarged 1 000 times. The second photograph is a transverse section through a piece of charcoal originating from the wood of an Acacia karoo tree. The enlargement is 50 times and allows the recognition of the distinctive arrangement of the vessels and rays in the wood. Studies such as these provide valuable information about the floral environment of a site at different times in the past. (Photograph: H. J. Deacon)

vicinity of the site in the past. Such information is obviously of considerable importance from an environmental point of view, and it is always necessary to check whether or not the patterns which emerge from faunal and pollen studies coincide.

Another form of botanical remains that commonly occurs in archaeological sites is charcoal. This material, apart from being used for radiocarbon dating, can also be subjected to microscopic study in an attempt to identify the various trees that existed in the past. Work along these lines is being undertaken at the Boomplaas site near Oudtshoorn, and the long sequence that has been disclosed is producing valuable information on changing vegetation patterns through time.

Plant remains more directly related to human dietary habits are also preserved in some sites. Pips, corm casings, and other materials illustrate the plant foods exploited by prehistoric people. At the De Hangen site large quantities of *Iris edulis* corm casings were recovered, and as this plant is most visible in the early summer months its occurrence at the site tended to support the evidence of seasonal occupation suggested by the dassie remains.

Wood and fibre were, of course, used in the past for the manufacture of various types of artefacts. Fragments of these, apart from being of cultural interest (as we discussed earlier), can also provide information about the exploitable plant resources of the past.

Seed impressions in fragments of pottery recovered at the Silverleaves site in the northern Transvaal have provided the first direct evidence for the cultivation of a domesticated plant in South Africa. Unfired and still damp clay pots were evidently placed there on a surface that had a few seeds scattered over it. These seeds were impressed into the clay but, of course, when the pots were fired the seeds were burnt out. The seed impressions, however, remained, and were later identified as being impressions of grains of millet (*Pennisetum americanum*).

Inorganic remains

Apart from the actual objects and distributions of objects preserved in archaeological sites, the deposit itself is of considerable interest to the archaeologist. Soil samples are regularly collected from archaeological sites for detailed laboratory analysis. These soil samples can provide information about the conditions under which the site formed. Was it wetter or drier than at present? Was the deposit formed by wind or by water action? Chemical testing can also throw light on how certain areas within the site were used. A high phosphate level, for example, may indicate an area where dung accumulated in the past and therefore where domestic animals were kept.

The wider framework: spatial analysis

Apart from studying the remains from within specific archaeological sites, archaeologists are also interested in the interrelationships between different kinds of sites, and the relationships between those sites and the general environment. A camp site or a village might, for example, be related to a nearby fish trap in a river or among rocks on the sea-shore, or it might be related to a pit-fall trap for hunting game, or to a nearby burial ground. Moreover, if the people under study were hunter-gatherers, they would have moved seasonally in response to fluctuations in the availability of important resources. To understand their annual cycle the archaeologist would have to identify all the types of sites related to that cycle. It might also be important for him to study the distribution of a particular type of architectural style or pottery style. In short, it is essential for the archaeologist to be concerned not only with individual sites, but also with the wider social and cultural relationships of these sites.

Environmental factors may, moreover, have had a profound influence on the distribution and development of different cultural patterns; and so by relating spatial patterning to environmental zonation the archaeologist can expect to gain some insight into these processes. Iron Age farming communities in South Africa settled only in the summer rainfall areas receiving more than about 400 mm per annum — drier areas were not suitable for cultivation without the irrigation schemes provided by modern technology.

The focus of archaeological analysis must therefore ultimately lie beyond single sites, in regional perspectives.

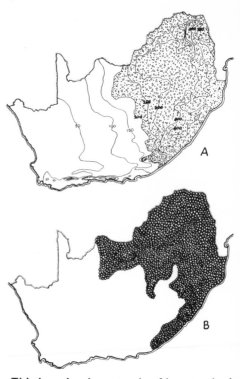

This is a simple example of how ecological factors can affect the distribution of cultural features. Map A shows the normal summer rainfall area in South Africa as well as the mean precipitation in millimetres for the period December to February. Map B shows the distribution of Iron Age settlement in South Africa. The close correlation between summer rainfall and Iron Age settlement is a reflection of the fact that these farmers were dependent upon crops which required more than a certain minimum of rainfall falling during the summer months.

The interpretation of archaeological data

Paradigms and models

The final step in the archaeological process is the interpretation of the data the archaeologist has amassed. What do all these data tell us about the past?

In truth, of course, archaeological interpretation has crept into the picture already. Although archaeological remains actually exist in an objective way, they cannot speak for themselves; the archaeologist must abstract his data and he is therefore already 'interpreting'. In this section, however, we shall be concerned with how the archaeologist puts his data together in a meaningful way.

There are two fundamental concepts which have to be appreciated if one is to make sense of the variety of interpretations, some of them conflicting, that appear in archaeological publications. The first of these concepts is *paradigm*.

All archaeologists operate within a particular paradigm. This means that they have certain explicit (or more often implicit) expectations with regard to the archaeological record. The archaeologist thinks within a particular logical framework, and it is this framework that provides the basis for the way in which he looks for and orders his data. This book has, for example, been written on the assumption that the archaeological record reflects the activities of man as a cultural being. Other archaeologists can, and do, take a somewhat different view. Some of the major paradigms current in archaeology today will be discussed below.

The second important concept to understand is *model*. A model is simply an hypothesis or theory constructed to explain a specific set of data. Many models may be generated within a particular paradigm to explain the phenomena recognised by that paradigm. Some approaches, by their very nature, make more use of models and model-testing than do other paradigms.

The cultural historical paradigm

Archaeologists who work within the cultural historical paradigm tend to view the cultural material recovered from the archaeological record as basically a reflection of the shared cultural beliefs and norms of vanished societies. Their main concern, therefore, is with the description of those cultural systems through time. Cultural historical archaeologists make extensive use of ethno-archaeology and history in an effort to find analogues that will help to explain the patterning which they find in the archaeological record. Some cynics say that this amounts to little more than 'ethnographic snap'! Despite this and other criticisms, however, there can be little doubt that the construction of a basic culture history for any area is an indispensable first step towards the development of what other archaeologists might regard as more 'sophisticated' paradigms.

The cultural processual paradigm

An important recent development within archaeology has been the emergence of the so-called 'new archaeology'. This approach has arisen as a result of the dissatisfaction of some archaeologists with the interpretations possible within the cultural historical paradigm. The 'new archaeologists' are more concerned with *process* in the archaeological record. They are interested, for example, in how and why change takes place, and in explaining why, in fact, stability or lack of change sometimes occurs. Processual archaeologists tend to view culture from an evolutionary perspective, which projects a dynamic view of systems in balance between forces generating variability and forces reducing variability. Processual archaeologists therefore seek explanations rather than descriptions. A characteristic of the cultural processual paradigm is the setting up and testing of models or hypotheses. Processual archaeologists may, for example, use ethnographic data but they would use such data not to look for analogies but to set up hypotheses about what might be expected in the archaeological record. The archaeological pattern may in fact turn out to be very different from the observed (ethnographic) pattern, and this would require explanation and may lead to the identification of processes not in operation in modern ethnographic data. The processual archaeologist would therefore emphatically deny that our knowledge of the past must be limited by what we know of the present. The ultimate goal of the cultural processual paradigm is the discovery of laws of human behaviour. Many archaeologists and anthropologists believe, however, that human behaviour is far too diverse to be 'predictable' in the usual scientific sense.

The ecological paradigm

Although ecological models feature in both the paradigms already discussed, it is possible to recognise a separate ecological paradigm. This paradigm differs from the cultural approaches in that it takes as its point of departure the ecology and environment of a given area. The concern here is with the way in which man has distributed himself around a landscape. What, for example, were the environmental factors that led to a particular settlement pattern? How does the environment permit or cause change? Why were certain site localities 'chosen'? These are some of the questions asked by ecological archaeologists. Many archaeologists attempt to construct models on the basis of the ecology of an area which 'predict' where sites might be expected to occur. The archaeologist then tests these ecological models by going into the field to discover whether or not the predicted pattern in fact exists. Ecological archaeology, of course, draws extensively on work carried out within the general ecological paradigm, which is so important in all the life-sciences today.

Views of the past in the future

It is important to remember that the paradigms currently in use do not form water-tight compartments. Cultural historical archaeologists must obviously consider environmental factors, just as the ecological archaeologist relies upon a knowledge of the cultural history of an area in order to know what to expect in the archaeological record. Even more important is the realisation that as archaeological research and science in general progress, new techniques and insights will open up possibilities not yet imagined. Consider, for example, the whole new world that was opened to science by the development of the microscope. Researchers were not only able to find many elusive answers, but also to formulate new and even more penetrating questions. And so it will be with archaeology as the discipline develops, and new methods and techniques are evolved. We may see things dimly now, but who knows what we shall find in the past in the future?

How can I get involved?

In South Africa all archaeological remains are protected by law and it is an offence to 'destroy, damage, excavate, alter, remove from its original site or export' any archaeological remains except in terms of a permit issued by the National Monuments Council. Such permits are normally only issued to suitably trained and qualified people.

In order to become professionally involved in archaeology it is necessary to obtain at least an Honours degree. Formal training in archaeology is offered by the Universities of Cape Town, Fort Hare, Pretoria, Stellenbosch and the Witwatersrand. The University of South Africa offers degree courses by correspondence.

The South African Archaeological Society (Private Bag X4, Leeusig, 8009), which has both amateur and professional members, exists to promote archaeology and disseminate archaeological information through its *Bulletin* and newsletter, *The Digging Stick*, published twice a year, as well as other publications issued at irregular intervals. The Society has, in addition, local branches in the Western Cape, Southern Cape, Natal and Transvaal, which organise regular lectures, outings and other archaeologically orientated activities. The Society always welcomes enquiries from anyone with an interest in archaeology.

Suggested reading

There are few books on archaeological methods and techniques that refer specifically to southern African conditions. The following more general books can, however, be recommended.

Deetz, J. *Invitation to Archaeology*. New York: The Natural History Press, 1967. (A very brief introduction available in paperback.)

Fagan, B. M. *In the Beginning*. Boston: Little, Brown, 1975.

Hole, F. & Heizer, R. F. *An Introduction to Prehistoric Archaeology*. New York: Holt, Rinehart & Winston, 1973.

Knudson, S. J. *Culture in Retrospect*. Chicago: Rand McNally, 1978.

Sharer, R. J. & Ashmore, W. *Fundamentals of Archaeology*. Menlo Park, California: Benjamin/Cummings, 1979. (These are comprehensive surveys of archaeological methods and techniques aimed at first-year university students.)

Binford, L. R. *In Pursuit of the Past*. London: Thames and Hudson, 1983. (Processual archaeology in action, with several case studies drawn from southern Africa.)

Some of the results of archaeological research in southern Africa are presented in the following books.

Inskeep, R. R. *The Peopling of Southern Africa*. Cape Town: David Philip, 1978. (A well-illustrated survey of the prehistory of southern Africa.)

Klein, R. G. (ed.) *Southern African Prehistory and Paleoenvironments*. Rotterdam: A. A. Balkema, 1984. (A comprehensive and well-documented summary for more specialised readers.)